W9-BRS-852

3o Day
ESSENTIALS
for
CAREER

30 Day ESSENTIALS for

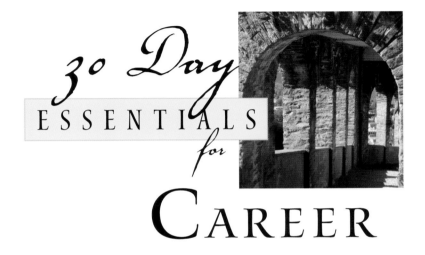

CAREER

JYOTISH NOVAK

CRYSTAL CLARITY PUBLISHERS
NEVADA CITY, CALIFORNIA

Copyright © 2004 by Crystal Clarity Publishers

All rights reserved
ISBN 1-56589-175-9

1 3 5 7 9 10 8 6 4 2

Design by Stephanie Steyer
Photography by Swami Kriyananda, Jyotish Novak,
        Robert Frutos and Stephanie Steyer

 Crystal Clarity Publishers   Phone: 800.424.1055 or 530.478.7600
14618 Tyler Foote Road   E-mail: clarity@crystalclarity.com
Nevada City, CA 95959   Website: www.crystalclarity.com

Printed in China

Library of Congress Cataloging-in-Publication Data
Novak, John (John Jyotish)
  30 day essentials for career / Jyotish Novak ; [design by Stephanie Steyer ; photography by Swami
Kriyananda... [et al.].
      p. cm. — (30 day essentials ; 2)
  Features inspirational advice and a suggested exercise for each day.
  ISBN 1-56589-175-9 (hard cover, number 2 in a series)
  1. Quality of work life. 2. Conduct of life. 3. Work — Psychological aspects. 4. Self-actualization (Psychology)
I. Title: Thirty day essentials for career. II. Title.
  HD6955.N68 2004
  650.14—dc22

                                2004014308

This book is dedicated to my teachers and my co-workers. They have shown me that life is an adventure and that work can be wonderful.

Many people see their job as something to be endured in order to get a paycheck. But so much more is possible from work: happiness, creativity, and self-expansion. To see your career only in terms of money is like a miner so intent on picking up flecks of gold from the gravel that he fails to notice that the hills above him are full of rich veins.

Over your lifetime you will likely spend more than 10,000 days at work. Don't waste such a precious opportunity for growth and fulfillment. Life is not like a race where the whole focus is on the finish line. Take pleasure in the journey itself. In the long run, how much you enjoy your job will largely determine how much you enjoy your life.

I was once volunteering to help rebuild houses in a community that had been destroyed by a forest fire. Many of the volunteers were, like me, less than accomplished carpenters. Due to mistakes, we were actually farther behind by noon than when we started the day. At lunchtime our crew leader made a comment that I have always remembered. He said, "Let's remember what's important. We're here to build character, not houses."

This book is meant to enrich your experience of work. You'll find attitudes and techniques that will help enhance your career and your life. There's also a practical exercise for each day. Try to absorb the attitudes and practice the exercises, and you will experience a personal transformation. Each day can be filled with the "gold" of increasing fulfillment, confidence, and contentment.

Review Your Goals

Take time today to review your goals. Step back from your daily routine and see life as a unified whole, with your career in proper balance. Ask yourself, "What do I really want in my life? Why have I chosen this particular job? How does my career relate to my deeper goals, to my personal fulfillment?" Knowing what you want from your career can help you be more effective.

Since we devote so much time to work, our job needs to offer more than just financial security. It should also provide a sense of fulfillment and personal growth. Life's goals can be attained only after they have been identified, so take a few minutes to write down what is most important to you. Once you know your priorities and keep them clear, you are on your way to a truly successful life.

Identify and
write down your
goals in life.

TRY THIS

See your success in inner rather than outer terms.

Success

The drive to succeed is a primal force — seen even at the cellular level. Success at work is vital to your sense of self-worth and fulfillment. Most people define success according to salary, title, or status — the rewards for hard work and dedication. We might call these the social symbols of success. But there is another, more important way to look at the subject. "Inner success" has little to do with rewards or recognition. It is defined by what you are rather than what you have. A truly successful person is happy and contented and lives according to his or her own principles. On his deathbed, not even a workaholic gasps out, "I wish I could have spent more time at the office." In the end, a successful life is judged by the simplest of questions: "Have I lived up to my ideals? Have I loved and been loved?"

Integrity

If there is a single quality that society needs today, it is integrity. The worlds of business and entertainment, and our culture in general, are crippled by a lack of morality. Yet, the struggle for virtue must be personal — it must begin with you. Don't sacrifice your integrity for a temporary advantage, because ultimately, how you work will help define who you will become. Never, but never, lie or cheat or intentionally hurt others. You shrivel with every dishonorable act. Loyalty to your business is important, but be more loyal to honesty itself. Men and women of absolute integrity develop an almost mystical power. It's as if the universe itself moves aside to let them pass. Think of great examples from history: Jesus, Buddha, or more recently, Lincoln, Einstein, and Mother Teresa. The shining example of their integrity has lit the way for countless millions. The same power that allowed them to change the world will help you to succeed in your own life, in your own career. When it is difficult to know what course to take, always choose the course that allows you to be a better human being.

TRY THIS

Act with absolute integrity in everything you do.

Then do the same tomorrow.

DAY 4 Excellence

Strive for excellence. Unless you aim for the heights you can never be more than mediocre. Yet excellence, like a mountain peak, is reached one step at a time — the determined acts daily of dedication. To achieve excellence, you need to develop the habit of doing even small tasks with great awareness. Each job has certain critical skills and tools you must learn in order to succeed. Take a moment to make an inventory of the basic requirements in your job, and then set out to master them. It will take study, determination, and practice, but unless you make the necessary effort you will never excel. No concert pianist ever walked onto the stage without countless hours of practice at the keyboard. Excellence also has a broader implication than just job skills. Strive for excellence in all areas of your life: physical, mental, emotional, and spiritual. In the final analysis, mastering yourself is your real job in life.

TRY THIS

Make a list of skills and qualities you need to excel.

~

TRY THIS

Accept absolute

responsibility for

what is yours.

Take Responsibility

The most prized workers in any company are those who can get the job done. Henry Ford valued responsibility above all else and always promoted those who expressed this rare quality. Accepting responsibility requires both strength of mind and strength of will. Once you accept an obligation, be willing to move mountains to accomplish it! Never try to shift your responsibility to someone else. Be like President Truman, who kept on his desk a plaque, which said in bold letters, "The Buck Stops Here!"

There is another, broader aspect to this subject. Accept personal responsibility for everything in your life — your health, your relationships, and your happiness. Only you are responsible for you! When you truly realize this, you will have the power to change your very destiny.

DAY 5

A positive
outlook creates
positive
magnetism,
which elevates
everyone
around you.

∽

TRY THIS

Look carefully at your team. Is there an atmosphere of harmony

and cooperation? If not, start to create it today.

❧

Cooperation

6

Observe how your thoughts and actions influence others. No individual, however talented, can achieve as much as a team of people, all focused on the same goal, and able to work together effectively. Cooperation is the glue that binds a group together. Teamwork creates harmony and helps neutralize the power games that so often ruin a work environment. Cooperation doesn't mean suppressing your talents, but rather weaving them into the fabric of a group, so that each person adds his special gifts. A truly aware person will be able to feel the energy field of a group and see how to draw out the best in each person. While group harmony is important, it is essential that you never surrender your sense of integrity in order to be popular.

One hallmark of genius is the ability to make connections where others see only separation. Be a force of friendship and cooperation. Treat everyone with respect and appreciation, and they'll gladly do their best. Relate to them with disrespect and condescension, and they will silently undercut you. Cooperation is like oil in an engine — be sure to add it on a regular basis, and you'll avoid a meltdown.

Communication

Unless you work in complete isolation, you need to be able to communicate effectively. An exchange of ideas requires not only the capacity to express your thoughts clearly but also the ability to listen to others. Learn to "hear" body language and the silent thoughts behind the words. Many people are keen to convey their own ideas but are too self-focused to actually listen to anyone else. There is a story about Theodore Roosevelt at a cocktail party who, as an experiment, went from person to person saying that he had just killed his mother. Each responded with a comment like, "Oh, isn't that nice. By the way, I've been meaning to ask you about my project."

Good communication with your co-workers requires daily attention; so make sure to connect regularly. Create an atmosphere where people feel that their ideas are welcome. Communication blossoms when people feel relaxed and appreciated. Keep your ears — and also your heart — open.

DAY 7

TRY THIS

Spend time really listening to the ideas of a co-worker.

✍

Increase Your Will Power

Will power (energy directed toward a specific goal) is one of the strongest forces on earth. Nothing can long resist energy applied with power and persistence. Will power is like a switch — the stronger your will, the more powerful the flow of energy. Weak or blocked energy will produce meager results, but a strong and focused will is like a powerful laser. It can bounce light off the moon or cut through any obstacle. To keep will power from seeming grim, think of it as willingness.

Positive enthusiasm will strengthen your willingness power. Here's a simple technique: Take on something that is easily within your capabilities and be sure to accomplish it. Gradually take on more and more difficult challenges, and make sure you always complete them. Eventually you'll find that you have tremendous energy — you can even draw the power of the universe to support your goals. Your willingness will help to infuse your co-workers with determination. This is how wars are won, and great companies built.

TRY THIS

Decide to accomplish a task and then Do It!

✌

TRY THIS

Act enthusiastic and be enthusiastic.

✍

Be Enthusiastic

Enthusiasm is essential to success. Many people stumble through life taking two steps forward and one step backward. Their efforts are blocked by a lack of intensity, almost as if they are embarrassed by accomplishment. Don't be afraid to let people see your excitement. Act enthusiastic even when others are not, and you'll be surprised at how easily they accept your ideas. Being positive unleashes your own strength and creativity and attracts help from other people. Here are three simple things you can do to increase your enthusiasm:

1) Express positive attitudes — not just with your thoughts, but also with your body language. Stand up straight, shoulders back, and take a few deep breaths. This enlists the powerful mind-body connection. It also sends a subtle message of strength to others around you.

2) Immediately throw out doubts or negative thoughts as soon as they enter your mind. Mentally affirm, "I am positive, energetic, enthusiastic."

3) Visualize the task before you. See it in a positive light and imagine yourself completing it easily and joyfully.

Create an aura

of concentration

at your desk or

workplace.

Learn to Concentrate

Learn to concentrate completely on the task before you. Your focus should be like a microscope, excluding all other thoughts and penetrating to the heart of the work at hand. Do just one task at a time, and stay with it until it is done — a scattered mind accomplishes nothing. Deep concentration activates your inner powers of inspiration. Einstein became so focused on his mathematical theories that he was often unaware of whether or not he had eaten. If you have a lengthy task, refresh your mind by taking a five or ten minute break every two hours, preferably in fresh air.

In your workplace it may be necessary to set aside certain times for concentrated work. Make sure your office communicates an aura of concentration that others feel and respect. Protect your space by socializing in a lunchroom or somewhere away from where you do your focused work. Remember, a focused mind can accomplish miracles.

DAY 10

All great
discoveries come
from intuition.

❧

Work Hard

There is no substitute for plain hard work. Lazy people do not succeed, nor are they happy, because both success and happiness require energy. Doing your job without intensity is a formula for failure. Edison said that genius is 10% inspiration and 90% perspiration. If you train yourself to break through resistance points, the inner temptation to give up, you'll find new strength flowing into you — a kind of second wind. One way to be a winner is to put energy into everything you do, even a small task like answering an email. Directing your energy, like balancing on a beam, is more a matter of focus than of effort. Tension just introduces friction into the system, so if you learn to relax, you'll be more effective. A champion marathoner must learn to stay relaxed even while putting out tremendous, sustained effort. Hard work is the foundation for victory.

TRY THIS

Put energy into even the small tasks you do today.

～

TRY THIS

Be conscious of projecting a field of positive magnetism around yourself.

࿇

Project
Magnetism

Laws of physics often have a human counterpart, and magnetism is expressed both in nature and in people. Physical magnetism is created when the molecules in a bar of iron are all aligned in one direction or when electricity flows through a wire. Human magnetism is created when the mind is focused on a single goal. In both cases, increasing the flow of energy amplifies the magnetism. Here is the law: The greater the flow of energy, the greater the power of magnetism. With every interaction, we unconsciously exchange magnetism, so it is important to be aware of this force when choosing your friends and business partners. If you consciously project magnetism, you can draw to yourself the people, ideas, and even the money you need. To increase your mental magnetism, you must clarify and empower your thoughts. Doubts, lethargy, or fuzzy thinking all weaken the flow. When you take on a task give it one hundred percent of your energy, and you will draw to yourself everything you need to succeed.

Develop Habits of Success

Habits can be great friends or fierce enemies; success requires good work routines. To create or destroy a habit, you must simply reprogram your brain patterns. When creating a new habit, it helps if you first clearly identify what you want to do. Visualize the new habit, mentally commit yourself, and determinedly brush aside all doubts that might oppose you. With deep commitment it is possible to start a good habit or drop a bad one immediately, but usually it takes some time. Try an experiment. Pick a habit that would be helpful in your work, say, keeping a clean desk. Now, for the next 30 days be sure to follow your new resolution. No exceptions. No excuses. After that time you will find that the new habit, like a young tree, has become rooted in your subconscious. Don't waste time with guilt or regret. To concentrate on forming good habits is far more effective than to fight bad ones, since a positive pattern cancels out a negative one. For instance, the habit of immediately returning calls will counter the habit of procrastination. By establishing a new, positive pattern you will automatically eliminate, or at least reduce, the old one. Your job will be easier and more fun if you make good habits your partner.

TRY THIS

Start one new positive habit and keep it up for 30 days.

∿

TRY THIS

Take an inventory of your work environment. Add the colors and items that
help empower you. Remove those that drain your energy.

〜

Enhance Your Environment

Your environment is more important than you realize. Science has shown that surroundings are powerful influencers of moods and behavior. Make sure that your workspace helps you feel good. Simple changes in color schemes or a rearrangement of furniture can improve your subliminal impressions and performance. For instance, a messy, cluttered environment tends to produce unfocused thoughts, while a clean area helps you concentrate. Color stimulates areas deep in the brain that effect mood. You don't need a high-priced consultant to improve your job performance; simply incorporate colors you find pleasing and energizing. Visualize yourself in an environment that empowers you. What colors do you see? Are there particular sounds or even scents that help create a sense of strength and well-being? Introduce some of these elements into your workspace; at the same time, be sure to remove things that subtly annoy you or bring you down. A few minutes spent consciously creating your environment can pay vast dividends in your energy and productivity.

14

Time Management

To be productive, you have to manage your time. Efficient people have an innate ability to prioritize their workload and do critical tasks first. Time management is a surprisingly easy skill to acquire; it just takes a little, well, time. Here's how: Spend five minutes at the start of each day to make, and prioritize, a list of what you want to accomplish. Some people make a simple list, while others prefer to assign a number: 1, 2, or 3, indicating the importance of each task. On Monday, do this for the entire week ahead. Every few weeks it is good to look at your long-range schedule to make sure important projects aren't getting sidetracked. To be effective, you'll have to ignore unnecessary demands and stick with your priorities. Use these same time management techniques to balance the different demands in your life. Don't allow precious months or years to slip by without paying attention to family, friends, and other activities that are important to you. Time management, like the turning of the seasons, allows your life to flourish and blossom.

TRY THIS

Spend five minutes to prioritize the demands of the day. Spend a few more

minutes to see how to balance the different elements in your life.

∽

Life reflects back
to us the kind
of energy that we
put out.

❧

Have Realistic Expectations

Be sure that your expectations, both for yourself and for others, are realistic and achievable. Unattainable goals cause discouragement, failure, and friction, poisoning the atmosphere in your workplace. If you lead others, be sure to clearly communicate not only the long-term goal, but also the steps along the way. It is good, when setting group goals, to enlist other members of your team. That way they feel a sense of commitment. Follow up by giving them the help they need to meet the objectives in a timely manner. And make it fun. Why take the joy out of work?

If you need to correct someone for not meeting a reasonable expectation, make your point clearly, quickly, and without emotional overtones. Then be sure to let them know that you appreciate areas where they are doing well. People are like plants; they grow when nourished but shrivel in harsh conditions. Having clear and reasonable expectations is vital to creating a successful working environment.

TRY THIS

Make sure that your expectations are realistic

and clearly communicated.

‫❧

TRY THIS

Do a routine

task in a

completely new

way.

↝

Be Creative

Creativity is one of the most important forces of nature, so if we aren't creative in our career, we'll end up feeling shrunken and unhappy. One way to expand your creativity is to do something new and different every day. Carry out even routine tasks in an inventive manner. To encourage a flow of creativity, keep your energy level high and expect a solution. Positive expectations, assuming that a solution already exists, help open an effortless flow of creative intuition. Creative geniuses often feel that they don't so much create their works as receive them. Mozart and Beethoven spoke of hearing melodies coming from a higher realm.

When approaching a problem, break free from old patterns and generate numerous, even unusual, solutions. Think outside the box. David Ogilvey, the famous advertiser, would create as many as twenty entirely different ideas for an ad campaign. Don't be too concerned about details at first, or you will stop your natural flow of inspiration. After the initial ideas have formed clearly, it is good to view them through the lens of common sense, the accumulated wisdom of ten thousand experiences. Step back from the flush of creativity and ask yourself, "Will it work?"

Visualization

Visualization is a surprisingly powerful tool. Studies showed that students in a gym class who simply visualized shooting free throws were nearly as successful as those who spent hours practicing. Watch Olympic athletes visualizing their routines before they compete. At work, you can use visualization to prepare for success — before making a sales presentation, for example, or talking with someone about a difficult situation. Visualization is also a wonderful way to create unity in a group. Try starting your next meeting with a guided visualization and you'll be surprised at how in sync the group becomes. On an individual level, visualization is a powerful tool in overcoming illness.

When you visualize, picture the activity or object very clearly in your mind's eye. It is even more powerful if you include other senses such as hearing, touch, taste, and smell. See and feel yourself going through the entire process in a completely successful manner. Repeating your visualization several times will help you program your subconscious mind and prepare you for success.

18

DAY

TRY THIS

Visualize your next important task before you do it.

‰

TRY THIS

Use patience in a situation where you might be tempted to be impatient.

∾

19

DAY

Patience &
Perseverance

No career can be successful without patience and perseverance. To achieve results you need to respect the natural rhythms of people and projects. Impatience simply adds tension, not efficiency, and is often just a veiled excuse to give up in a difficult situation. Patience need not imply passivity. A teacher was hurrying to get to his lecture on time. His companion said, "Don't be nervous." The teacher replied, "You can run calmly or you can run nervously, but not to run when you're late is to be lazy." The active side of patience is perseverance, which is required in all large projects. Discipline yourself to stay with a task until it is finished, even if it takes great will power. In the end, all obstacles will crumble when faced with patience and determination. In working with others, patience can mean the difference between making friends or creating enemies. Accept people as they are, not as you wish them to be. When you support others with patience and faith in their potential, you open the door for miracles to occur.

Inner Strength

Many people float through life like jellyfish, waiting for circumstances to bring them what they want. In the workplace, a passive strategy typically leads to failure. Develop inner strength and you will acquire great powers of accomplishment. When you deeply believe in a project or a goal, let nothing keep you from accomplishing whatever you set out to do. Even failure, if it doesn't break your spirit, is but a steppingstone to success. Yet, even the strongest person has limits. True inner strength comes from aligning yourself with the laws of the universe. Mahatma Gandhi transformed the entire nation of India by becoming a living example of the principle of non-violence. You, too, can accomplish great deeds if you get yourself out of the way — a window that is crystal clear allows the sun's undiminished light to shine through. Inner strength increases when you forget yourself and focus entirely on what needs to be accomplished.

TRY THIS

Forget about

yourself so that

the power of your

inner strength

can shine.

In the end, all
obstacles will
crumble when
faced with
patience and
determination.

Happiness Is Within

Happiness is a state of mind that doesn't depend upon circumstances or conditions. You create expectations and then choose to make yourself happy or unhappy depending upon whether or not they are fulfilled. But no thing can make you unhappy — unless you give it the power to control your mind. One of the great delusions of modern times is the belief that mere possessions have the capacity to bestow happiness. In fact, happiness is more at home with simplicity than with abundance; it comes, in large part, from simply accepting and enjoying things for what they are. Happiness thrives in a mind that is unattached, while bad moods come from the accumulation of small disappointments and unfulfilled expectations. Train yourself to see the positive side of situations; laugh with people not at them. Here are three simple steps to lasting happiness:

1) Accept whatever comes to you as your own.

2) Consciously decide to be happy, especially when circumstances try to pull you down.

3) Understand that the surest path to happiness is to help others to be happy also.

TRY THIS

Choose to be

happy.

DAY 21

TRY THIS

Meditate.

∽

Meditation

Meditation is, perhaps, the most beneficial habit you can possibly develop. Practiced by millions of business people, athletes, and spiritual seekers, it will improve all areas of your life. Calming and concentrating your mind allows you to get in touch with your inner well of strength, calmness, and joy. Inner silence can be a refuge to counteract the stresses of work, but meditation is much more than just a refuge. Spiritually, meditation helps you to expand your sense of self beyond your body and personality, and to experience your connection with infinity.

Meditation is simple: Sit upright and relax your body. Now relax your mind by letting go of thoughts about the past or future. Concentrate your attention at the point between the eyebrows. Observe your breath as it flows in and out. If your mind wanders, simply bring it back to watching the breath. When you are relaxed and concentrated, look into the light in your forehead. Feel it filling your body; then feel it expanding to connect you with the light that pervades all that is. Continue meditating for as long as it is enjoyable. End by radiating waves of light and peace from your heart to your family, friends, strangers and all who dwell on this earth.

Intuition

Most decisions are made from the level of the conscious logical mind, which approaches a problem like a puzzle. The "reasonable" approach relies upon habit and usually recycles variations of past solutions. But, each of us also has the power of intuition, which transcends the rational mind and gives fresh solutions — often ones of startling brilliance. All great discoveries come from intuition.

Here's how you can enhance your inner guidance. First, intuition needs a quiet, focused, receptive mind. Intuition speaks to us in a whisper, working more through feeling than intellect. The calm attentiveness of meditation is especially fertile soil. Define your question clearly; then simply hold the problem up and expect a solution. Usually a response will appear quickly. If no answer comes, try posing two alternatives. The right solution should produce a positive, but calm, feeling in the heart. It is very important not to have an emotional commitment to a particular resolution or you will block your intuition. Confidence in your intuitive powers will grow as you begin acting on your inner guidance. As you get more in touch with this inner power, you can trust it more completely. Finally you will realize that it is your surest guide, more powerful by far than mere logic.

TRY THIS

Clear your mind, and let intuition be your guide.

⸎

TRY THIS

Realize that what you give, you will receive.

ꙅ

The Law of Reciprocity

Always be guided by integrity and morality. One of the fundamental laws of the universe is The Law of Reciprocity, known as "karma" in the teachings of the East. It says that life reflects back to us the kind of energy that we put out, just as a mirror reflects back the color and intensity of the light it receives. Give love, kindness, and compassion, and the world will return these to you. Build your career upon a ruthless disregard of others, and the universe will mirror callousness back to you. Once we understand this principle, it becomes clear that the way we perform our work is more important than what we achieve. Our most important job is to become the kind of person we want to be. Our career is simply a means to that end. It is not so important to please others, but it *is* vital to follow our own sense of righteousness. Right action is the guiding principle for untold millions, and it should be the bedrock of your career. Jesus taught, as the most important rule of human interaction, "Do unto to others as you would have them do unto you."

DAY 24

Appreciation

America's best companies have found that the single most important ingredient for success is to treat their employees respectfully. When workers are treated with appreciation and respect, they feel empowered. Create a corporate culture of appreciation and you will reap abundant benefits through dedication and loyalty. When appreciation is absent, a company is like a garden without sunlight — nothing grows.

Find an appropriate way to express your appreciation to others in your work group — a kind word or note of thanks will accomplish more than a dozen reprimands. Appreciation also helps form bonds of trust and openness, so that people are receptive to suggestions for improvement. When working with others, always remember that people are more important than things.

TRY THIS

Express your appreciation to those around you.

Accept people
as they are, not
as you wish
them to be.

Even-Mindedness

Even-mindedness is a key to so much in life. Many people are like emotional yo-yos, up one moment and down the next. You can calm the emotional roller coaster by accepting things as they are, rather than rejecting life's experiences because they are not what you want them to be. If you become too elated over success or cast down by setbacks, you are certain to become moody; and since negative emotions are contagious, you can spoil your work environment. When you over-react, you take away the emotional space others need. Stay steady, do your best, and let results take care of themselves.

The key to even-mindedness is to calm the reactive process. Catch yourself as soon as you start to react to a situation, while you still have time to control your mood swings. Control your mind with the immediate, decisive resolution to be even-minded and cheerful. It will help if you take time regularly to be quiet and to be in nature. Too much stimulation, like wind on a lake, creates ripples of turmoil in your mind. Remain even-minded in all circumstances, and you will be able to sail the ship of your life cheerfully over all seas, rough and calm alike.

TRY THIS

Act; don't react. Be even-minded and cheerful no matter what happens.

‿

Think of three people and three things for which you are grateful.

Gratitude

Gratitude opens us to rays of positive energy. How much energy we waste by grumbling about what life brings us! The habit of complaining shuts off the flow of energy and creativity, and leaves us feeling bitter and exhausted. Gratitude is the antidote to this pernicious pattern. It opens us up to a positive flow of grace and gives us the ability to grow from every experience. Be thankful for everything — even difficulties help you to develop strength and determination.

Gratitude will make the world come alive. George Washington Carver, the great botanist, said, "Anything in nature will speak to you if you love it enough." He was talking about plants, but it is even truer when dealing with people. People perk up when they sense they are in the presence of a grateful and open heart. Ask this simple question: Do you prefer to spend time with someone who is constantly complaining or with someone who is happy and grateful to be with you? Be grateful, and you will be magnetic.

D A Y 27

Work as Service

This simple shift of attitude can improve the whole experience of your job: See your work as service. Think about what you give, rather than what you get. Contentment comes automatically when you forget about yourself, while virtually all unhappiness stems from too much self-involvement. Self-forgetfulness and self-expansion always lead to happiness. Here's a question: Think about people you know who are truly happy. Are they focused on themselves or on others?

As a life strategy, you will find that you are happier when you help others to be happy. Fulfillment increases when you see your career as an opportunity to serve the world. Try adding some public service to the routine of your life, and you'll be amazed at what a sense of satisfaction will come! Often the most fulfilling kind of service is done secretly or anonymously.

TRY THIS

Do an act
of service for
which you expect
no reward except
the joy of
serving.

TRY THIS

Think about who you want to be in five years.

৵

Build Your Character;
Build Your Career

Your real job in life is self-development. As you build a career, you gradually define your character. Most people worry about what their salary or position will be in the future, but a more valid question would be, "What qualities do I want to have in five years?" Your career is the canvas on which you will create that person. Here are six key character traits that everyone should strive for:

Integrity — Be the kind of person you would want your son or daughter to marry.

Harmony — Your career should create a circle of friends, not an army of enemies.

Inner Strength — Be like an oak, strong and flexible enough to weather any storm.

Focus — Make your mind a powerful laser, able to cut through all difficulties.

Creativity — Become a flowing fountain of new ideas and fresh energy.

Happiness — Be filled with delight for life, sharing your joy with everyone.

DAY

29

DAY Have Fun

30

Life is a quest for happiness. It is important that we find enjoyment in our work since it takes up such a large part of the day. A positive and happy attitude makes our minds and bodies function better, and we're much more effective at our job. Laughter has been found to be a great healer — a medicine you should take daily. Sometimes we just need to sit back and have a good belly laugh at life. True joy comes not from circumstances, but from our very nature. Stop occasionally, close your eyes, take a deep breath, and decide to be positive. A positive outlook creates positive magnetism, which elevates everyone around you. Develop a light "specific gravity" — so that you float like a cork on the waves of life. Especially when you are down, try to associate more with those who instinctively live with a light consciousness. Life is too short — and the workday too long — not to fill it with fun.

TRY THIS

Have fun!

❧

When you
support others
with patience and
faith in their
potential, you
open the door for
miracles to occur.

❧

Other titles in the 30-Day Essentials series:

30-*Day Essentials for Marriage* by Jyotish Novak

30-*Day Essentials for Health & Healing* by Jyotish Novak

Also by Jyotish Novak

How to Meditate: A Step-by-Step Guide to the Art and Science of Meditation

Meditation Therapy for Relationships (video)

Meditation Therapy for Stress & Change (video)

Meditation Therapy for Health & Healing (video)

Additional books from Crystal Clarity Publishers

Money Magnetism by J. Donald Walters

The Art of Supportive Leadership by J. Donald Walters

Secrets of Leadership by J. Donald Walters

Secrets of Prosperity by J. Donald Walters

Secrets of Winning People by J. Donald Walters

Secrets of Success by J. Donald Walters

Intuition for Starters by J. Donald Walters

Music to Relax, Uplift, and Inspire™ from Clarity Sound & Light

Relax: Meditations for Piano by David Miller

Relax: Meditations for Flute & Cello by Sharon Brooks and David Eby

The Mystic Harp by Derek Bell

Mystic Harp 2 by Derek Bell

For a free Crystal Clarity catalog, or to place an order,

please call 800.424.1055 or 530.478.7600

Or visit our website: www.crystalclarity.com